HEIRLOOM ROSES

HEIRLOOM ROSES

by rayford clayton reddell

photographs by saxon holt

CHRONICLE BOOKS

SAN FRANCISCO

Library of Congress Cataloging-in-Publication Data:
Reddell, Rayford Clayton.
Heirloom roses / by Rayford Clayton Reddell; photographs by Saxon Holt.
p.   cm.   Includes index.   ISBN 0-8118-2254-0 (hc)
1. Roses—Heirloom varieties. 2. Roses—Heirloom varieties—Pictorial Works.
I. Title.
SB411.R3925   1999   635.9'33734—dc21   98-19183 CIP

Printed in Singapore

Cover and book design by Gregory Design, San Francisco

The Photographer wishes to thank those who grew the roses. Garden Valley Ranch, Gregg Lowery and
Phillip Robinson of Vintage Gardens, Joyce Dimitz of Heritage Roses of Tanglewood Farm,
Louise Clements of Heirloom Old Garden Roses, Korbel Champagne Cellars, Phil Edinger, Michael Bates,
Freeland Tanner, Eleanor Moscow, Katie Trefethen, Empire Mine State Park, John Dallas,
Filoli Gardens, Jim and Dotty Walters, Diane and Jonathan Spieler, and Ann Leyhe for general assistance.

Distributed in Canada by Raincoast Books
8680 Cambie Street
Vancouver, British Columbia V6P 6M9

10   9   8   7   6   5   4   3   2   1

Chronicle Books
85 Second Street
San Francisco, CA 94105

www.chroniclebooks.com

This book is dedicated to the memory of Gerd Perkins,

who knew roses inside out, but especially the Heirlooms.

I never properly thanked her for sharing her heartfelt knowledge.

TABLE OF CONTENTS

INTRODUCTION

When I started growing roses, I had no clue what I was getting myself into, certainly not that the flower would ultimately consume my life. In those salad days, I asked only that whatever roses I took the trouble to grow bloomed their heads off; I wanted gratification, plenty of it. Consequently, my affair with roses began exclusively with modern varieties that bloomed steadily from May through October.

Over the next five or six years, I evaluated new varieties, constantly improving my habits of cultivating them. In what seemed like no time, I ran out of space in my San Francisco garden and, encouraged by the prospects of selling garden roses for a living, I went commercial and began growing garden roses for the wholesale cut-flower trade. The property I claimed home for my expanded rose collection is in Petaluma, California, a rural market town 40 miles north of San Francisco. The climate is nearly identical to that in the City, except that in summer the days are considerably warmer (although nights are just as chilly).

Once I had 8,000 rosebushes and a business going, I had time to learn why everyone made such a fuss over heirloom roses and I planted some in the landscape. I also had the opportunity to read up on the development of the genus Rosa.

The more I read, the more confused I became. Sure, I understood that Species roses once grew wild and that would-be hybridizers began messing around with their pollen, thereby producing new families, but I couldn't for the life of me figure out which clan came first or in what precise order.

Eventually I did, and I now understand that the horticultural progression of the genus Rosa *couldn't be less complicated, and that's the intent of this little book—to demystify the historical development of roses from the time they grew wild until breeders hybridized the first modern rose in 1867.*

'celestial'

1

S P E C I E S   R O S E S

No one is absolutely certain when or exactly how roses first developed, but everyone from archae-
ologists to botanists agrees that it was long before humans existed (according to fossil evidence
discovered in Colorado and Oregon, perhaps as long as 32 million years ago). To date, nearly
200 distinctly different species of roses have been identified and named.

Wild roses, as Species roses are commonly known, have diverse growing habits, varying from upright bushes to Ramblers and Climbers. Although color varied widely among early wild roses, their flowers didn't—single blossoms with five (sometimes four) petals. Wild roses weren't named, of course; that was not to occur until the 18th century, when the Swedish botanist Carolus Linnaeus established the binomial nomenclature that is the basis of modern plant taxonomy.

Species roses are divided into four groups by their place of origin—America, Europe, the Middle East, and Oriental Asia. Plant characteristics and bloom color vary widely.

'rosa carolina'

Compared with their European cousins, roses native to America are relatively low growing (almost always under 5 feet) and restricted in color range (primarily shades of pink). On the other hand, roses native to America are far more attractive in fall than are their European kin—the foliage turns autumnal shades and hips are plentiful.

American wild roses were often nicknamed for where they grew best, more specifically for their ability to tolerate seemingly undesirable soil conditions. For instance, the rose now known as *R. palustris* used to be known as the swamp rose because it thrived even in bogs. Similarly, what is now properly *R. setigera* was once merely the prairie rose.

Roses native to America made another gift to rosedom in that many grew relatively free of thorns. *R. blanda* was called the smooth rose long before it got its proper name. Similarly, both *R. carolina* and *R. foliolosa* are virtually thornless.

Although considered native to America, *R. nitida* is also distributed widely over Canada. Wherever it thrives, bushes are short and stems are thin, but the delicate foliage turns bright crimson in fall and shrubs sport oval hips that are tiny but plentiful and bristly.

'rosa nitida'

Roses native to Europe exhibit one of two distinguishing characteristics: either a gargantuan growth habit or favorably scented foliage. Also, their hips are prized as a particularly rich source of vitamin C.

R. canina, commonly known as the dog rose, is the most ubiquitous wild rose in all of Europe. Owing to its gangly growth habits (often beyond 10 feet), *R. canina* is most often planted in fields for windbreaks or as a hedgerow to separate grazing pastures. Despite of its hell-bent-for-survival growth habits, blossoms are delicate and nicely scented, as is the foliage. Because of the agreeable growth habits of *R. canina*, it was once used as rootstock for budding new varieties onto.

Equal in growth aspirations, albeit in a different direction, is *R. arvensis*, better known as the field rose. Because it prefers to hover close to the ground (or to trail along low fences), *R. arvensis* was the trailblazer to many a modern Ground Cover rose.

An apple scent predominates among European Species roses, and it's more often harbored in foliage rather than in blossoms. In *R. eglanteria*, for instance, the sweetly scented pale pink flowers are secondary to the intensely fragrant foliage. When crushed, leaves smell exactly like green apples. Bushes know no shame when it comes to size, easily reaching 15 feet. Hip production is astounding.

R. villosa also produces foliage famous for its scent of apples, but this time of ripe (rather than green) apples. The hips of *R. villosa* are even shaped like apples, crimson ones; they're also meticulously and perfectly symmetrically dotted with bristles.

'rosa canina and rosa eglanteria'

No wild roses made a stronger specific contribution to rosedom than did these Species roses. Wild roses native to the Middle East blossomed in a color unseen elsewhere—yellow, and bright yellow at that.

The palest of the group is *R. ecae*. Native to Afghanistan, *R. ecae* bears blossoms that are buttercup-yellow. Shrubs are composed of thorny brown wood and foliage is feathery.

As rich a yellow as one could hope to see, and certainly the most famous rose native to the Middle East, is *R. foetida*, which grows to 8 feet (taller if perfectly content) and has chestnut brown stems and black thorns.

Some years after it first grew wild (anyone's guess exactly when), *R. foetida* developed a sport (a spontaneous mutation). Instead of yellow blossoms, *R. foetida bicolor* (ubiquitously known as 'Austrian Copper') produces flowers that are an eye-blinking combination of copper and orange.

R. hemisphaerica, native to Southwest Asia, is commonly known as the sulphur rose and not only for its color. Although blossoms distinguish themselves by being double (as opposed to the more typical five-petaled flowers), their vaguely sulphuric aroma is off-putting.

'austrian copper'

Despite the fact that the contribution of yellow to the world of roses has certainly proved to be important, the gift was not entirely free. With it came an ailment known as blackspot, a persistent modern-rose disease all too familiar to gardeners in damp climates.

oriental asian species roses

Having saved the best for last, I can tell you that Species roses from Oriental Asia have made more important contributions to roses as we now know them than have those of any other place of origin. More than their violetlike scent and extended range of color, several of these roses possessed the most enviable of all qualities in a rose: an ability to repeat flowering during a growing season.

Although they bloom but once each season, the four members of the *R. banksiae* are the most famous of all roses from Oriental Asia. All have gargantuan growth habits and blossoms that smell of violets; they differ only in the form of their white or yellow flowers. *R. banksiae normalis* blossoms with single white flowers and *R. banksiae lutescens* with single yellow flowers. Double white flowers occur on *R. banksiae banksiae*, whereas *R. banksiae lutea* has double, butter-yellow blooms.

R. moschata, the original musk rose (so named because of its unmistakable musklike scent), was thought to be lost until 1963, when Graham Stuart Thomas, England's rose wizard, discovered a plant of the true species. A relatively short climber,

'lady banks'

R. moschata rarely grows taller than 10 feet, but blossoms, which begin life beige and eventually turn white, first appear in summer and flowering persists well into fall.

China, Japan, and Korea were also home to *R. rugosa*, a particularly winter-hardy Species rose that parented many a modern hybrid. Not only are *R. rugosa* and its offspring hardy, their foliage is tough as nails and the colors of their blossoms range from pure white to purplish red. Blooms are followed by tomato-shaped hips that are said to be richer in vitamin C than those of any other rose.

Ever since its discovery in eastern Asia in the 19th century, *R. multiflora* has been a favored rose even though its period of flowering (early summer) is over not long after it begins. Its popularity is based on the fact that when it does blossom, it's a blooming fool (up to 100 separate flowers in a cluster of blooms) and because it eagerly forms a root system so prodigious that it's become a favorite rootstock for budding modern rose hybrids onto.

'rosa moschata'

2

A N T I Q U E   R O S E S

Species roses continued to flourish for millions of years, steadily branching out from their original points of origin, but it was not until the Renaissance that new varieties of roses emerged. Then, determined to create beauty everywhere, including in the garden, aficionados finally turned their attention to improving plant forms.

Antique roses comprise five families that had established themselves as identifiable separate classes before the end of the 18th century: Gallicas, Damasks, Albas, Centifolias, and Mosses.

The vast majority of antique roses bloom only once each year, most often in early summer. When they do blossom, however, their floral display is stellar. So are the shrubs on which they grow—typically to 5-foot heights with half as much girth.

Unlike modern hybrid roses praised for their lovely buds, antique roses are prized for their mature blossoms. Buds, in fact, are often downright disappointing—cuppy or bull-nosed. As petals mature, however, the majestic blooms begin to quarter or swirl their petalage across blossoms the size of dinner plates.

'charles de mills'

The Gallicas are thought to be the oldest of all antique roses, dating back to Greek and Roman heydays, long before the French gave the family its name. Two characteristics best describe Gallica roses: deep coloring and intense fragrance.

By far the most famous of the Gallica family of roses is *R. gallica 'Officinalis'*, also known as the apothecary rose because its petals were once more praised for medicinal values than for beauty. However best appreciated, *R. gallica 'Officinalis'* produces sweetly scented, semidouble, crimson flowers with bright golden stamens on shrubs that arch gracefully in support of abundant dark green foliage.

The only Gallica rose giving 'Officinalis' a run for its money is its own sport (spontaneous mutation). *R. gallica versicolor*, ubiquitously known as 'Rosa Mundi', is a multicolored version of its parent. Blooms, no two alike but all fragrant, are basically blush white, then striped randomly with crimson, light purple, and pink.

The largest and most spectacular blossoms of all Gallicas are produced on the vigorous 'Charles de Mills'. Although fragrance is only mild, mature blossoms are so meticulously formed with intricately quartered maroon-to-purple petals that they look hand-fashioned.

Another Gallica low on fragrance but high on popularity is 'Empress Josephine', the hybrid chosen to bear the name of the greatest benefactress to roses, ever. As if to compensate for her scentlessness, the Empress pulls out all the stops

'cardinal de richelieu'

where showiness is concerned. The wavy petals composing each bloom are stiff with substance. Although blossoms are basically deep rose, each petal is veined randomly with lavender striations. Bushes may sprawl, but they're always richly foliated.

'Cardinal de Richelieu' is not only among the darkest of all Gallica roses, it's virtually as dark as any rose of any age. Buds that begin life deep pink mature to deep purple blossoms that reflex their petals into ball-shaped blossoms. Be forewarned that rainfall during bloom cycles badly discolors flowers. Even the soggiest of blossoms are intensely fragrant, however.

Many striped roses have come along since 'Camaieux', but none is finer or more richly fragrant. The base color of the blossoms is creamy white, but each petal is striped first with crimson, which turns to purple and finally to lilac. Bushes are just as wide as they are tall.

Rose antiquarians argue to this day whether or not 'Complicata' is a Gallica rose or a hybrid of *R. macrantha*, a Species rose that 'Complicata' vaguely resembles. I march with the Gallica group.

Among the armloads of pink five-petaled roses with golden yellow stamens, what sets 'Complicata' apart is a halo of white formed at the base of each petal. Although blossoms adamantly appear but once a year, they do so in astounding numbers. Plants are equally stubborn about their determination to thrive even in seemingly inclement conditions.

'complicata'

damask roses

Historians agree that the first Damask roses were cultivated in Persia and further that the first of the family resulted from a cross between a Gallica rose and *R. phoenicea*, a wild species native to the region.

Damask roses differ from Gallicas in that they are somewhat taller and their shrubs are looser in form; their wood is also considerably thornier. Almost all Damask roses are powerfully fragrant and blossom in pale colors from off-white to shell pink.

My personal pet of the Damask family is 'Madame Hardy', a truly classic old rose named for the wife of the head gardener to Empress Josephine. Bushes are vigorous but graceful growers. Still, because of their familial tendency to become loose, they look best in the landscape when massed in groups of three or five, where sprawling growth from one plant can spill over onto its neighbors to form a billowing, yet uniform, mound.

Blossoms are a marvel to watch mature. Cupped buds gradually flatten and reflex their petals, eventually revealing a green button-eyed center. Although buds have a pink blush to their outer petals, mature blossoms are gleaming white. Perfume is classic old rose with a hint of lemon.

'madame hardy'

Obviously closely related to 'Madame Hardy' is 'Madame Zoetmans', whose plants are more diminutive and whose blossoms are similarly colored, formed, and perfumed, but less prolific.

A clear favorite among the Damask family is 'Celsiana'. Bushes are notably graceful; so are the nodding blossoms. Petals start out dark pink, then fade to pale pink and near-white. As expected, blooms are sharply fragrant; the surprise comes with the petals, which, with their crumpled texture, resemble antique silk.

Historians pronounce 'York and Lancaster' an important member of the Damask family, although the story isn't exactly true that members of the opposing families waging the Wars of the Roses each took a blossom from a single bush—one red and one white—because 'York and Lancaster' produces no red roses; only pink and white, more frequently a combination of the two. No matter what the color, fragrance is strong.

'La Ville de Bruxelles' is a favored Damask among those devoted to oversized blossoms. Not only are the blooms huge, their outer petals reflex to make way for the intricately segmented petals within. Fragrance is downright decadent.

'la ville de bruxelles'

As with Damask roses, Alba roses came to be from the hands of Mother Nature, who mixed pollen from *R. damascena bifera* and the European Species rose *R. canina*. Since this fortuitous natural hybridization took place early in the 18th century, Linnaeus, the Swedish father of botany, was given the honor of naming the family. As the very name suggests, Albas are predominantly white, sometimes slightly off-white, but rarely darker than light pink.

The growth pattern of Alba roses is unmistakable. Once called tree roses because they grow so tall (often to heights of more than 6 feet), Albas have two other enviable qualities: they are adamantly resistant to winter and they tolerate more shade than does any other family of roses.

Surely the pride of the Alba family is 'Maiden's Blush', known in France as 'Cuisse de Nymphe' because its color is said to resemble that of the thigh of an aroused nymph. Although it's known by less provocative names elsewhere, 'Maiden's Blush' is a favorite everywhere roses grow.

I believe the secret is in the loosely double, blush-pink blossoms. Although they're only moderately sized, when blooms mass themselves in sprays (which they persistently do), the flowering effect is massive. As blooms mature, petals reflex and soften in color, but retain sharp fragrance.

'madame plantier'

Foliage is typical of the Alba family—gray-green and abundant. Shrubs may reach only 5 feet, but they arch their graceful stems almost as wide.

'Madame Legras de St. Germain' distinguishes herself from other Alba roses by growing relatively thornlessly. More important, her blossoms mature into the most perfect floral domes imaginable. Blooms are creamy white (fading with age), heavily petaled, and deeply scented. An aspiring grower, with an assist of proper support, 'Madame Legras de St. Germain' can be trained to climb up to 15 feet.

If climbing Alba roses appeal to you, have a look at 'Madame Plantier', which, when grown as a shrub, requires a 6-foot-round space regardless of how tall it eventually becomes. Blossoming consists of showers of small, sweetly fragrant, creamy white blossoms with a green button eye. When this Alba is trained with supports, an even finer floral display is available.

'Celestial' is a well-named Alba rose, both because its scent is heavenly and because its bush has lofty aspirations (easily to 5 feet and just as wide). The soft pink blooms are composed of sweetly scented, elegantly shaped petals.

R. alba semi-plena is commonly known as the 'White Rose of York' because the York family supposedly adopted it as their symbol during their War of the Roses. Whether or not that's true, the rose would have been a fine choice, seeing that it produces masses of soft white blossoms with fat, butter-yellow, stamen-packed centers on a particularly elegant, tall, trouble-free bush.

'white rose of york'

Blossoms of *R. alba semi-plena* are so packed with perfume that they were once widely cultivated in Bulgaria for the production of attar of roses.

centifolia roses

Rose antiquarians and plantsmen still argue vehemently about the origin of Centifolia roses. It would be convenient if a species rose named *R. centifolia* ever existed, but present-day plant pathologists assure us that none ever did. What is patently clear, however, is that the Dutch are credited with the development of Centifolias. Working with varieties that were known simply as cabbage roses, during the 17th century the Dutch introduced more than 200 new Centifolias. Their motivation was high because no flowers were more highly esteemed by artists for floral subjects in their paintings.

The majority of Centifolia roses are some shade of pink, but a few extend the color range to include mauve and purple. Almost all members of the family are both strongly fragrant and heavily petaled.

Although 'Centifolia' is merely a varietal (not a Species) rose, it nevertheless is quintessential because it embodies the qualities most closely associated with the family at large—large, rich pink, heavily petaled blooms with classic Old Rose perfume growing on a strong yet graceful, thorny bush.

'chapeau de napoleon'

My personal favorite among the Centifolias is 'Fantin-Latour', named for the 19th-century French artist famed for his paintings of flowers, most often roses, usually Centifolias.

Blossoms of 'Fantin-Latour' are a marvel to watch as they mature. Buds are cuppy and first appear with little promise of anything dramatic taking place. Then, as they age, petals reflex and segment themselves around a button-eyed center. The outer petals are blush pink, while the inner petals are deeper pink. Compared with other Centifolias, 'Fantin-Latour' is only moderately fragrant, but the perfume is sophisticated.

Perhaps it's the bushes on which 'Fantin-Latour' grows that make the variety so endearing. They're moderately tall (to 5 feet), slender rather than rotund, and well cloaked in dark green, smooth foliage.

'Chapeau de Napoleon' is so named because its gigantic sepals (leaflike coverings of rosebuds) compress petals into what looks like a three-cornered cocked hat. As the petals mature and force the sepals downward, blossoms reveal their true Centifolia heritage, becoming outlandishly large yet retaining fragrance.

Particularly floriferous for a Centifolia, 'Paul Ricault' also enjoys an extended period of bloom. Blossoms are fully double, deep rose, and richly fragrant. Bushes are vigorous.

'de meaux'

Speaking of vigor, no Centifolia I know can top 'Tour De Malakoff', which spreads its limbs so far that they demand support. The bonus comes with the blossoms, which are prolific, deeply scented, and intensely colored with shades of crimson, magenta, purple, and violet.

Centifolia roses are available in miniature version, too. 'De Meaux' is surely the most celebrated diminutive member of the family, not only because its warm pink flowers, up to 1 inch wide, are deliciously fragrant but also because they occur on well-behaved, short shrubs massed in small, light green leaves.

'Petite de Hollande', another miniature Centifolia, differs from 'De Meaux' in that its bushes are larger and its blossoms a softer shade of pink. Otherwise, fragrance is just as expected and foliage is appropriately sized for the plants on which it grows.

moss roses

Although the first reliable spotting of a true Moss rose occurred in Carcassonne, France, in 1696, it took another 150 years for the family to catch on. Then English Victorians could not get their fill and Moss roses were subjected to all sorts of breeding lines, resulting in varieties that ranged in color from white to maroon and in growth habits from miniatures to skyscrapers. Because parents chosen for hybridizing new varieties sometimes included reblooming varieties, several Moss roses were introduced that blossomed almost continuously during each season of growth.

'communis'

As the family name indicated, Moss roses display conspicuous mosslike growth that often appears on stems, calyxes, sepals, and even leaflets of the plants on which they flower. Degree of mossing varies almost as widely as color and growth patterns—usually soft, often prickly, but sometimes piercingly sharp.

The 'Common Moss' rose, also known as 'Old Pink Moss' or 'Communis', is thought to be the original Moss rose from which all other varieties descended. 'Common Moss' is said to be a "well-mossed" member of the family, implying that "mossy" growths are apparent on both the plant and its blossoms.

Shrubs of 'Common Moss' grow to moderate (4-foot) heights and about half as wide. Plentiful, tough, disease-resistant foliage is midgreen, and blossoms are midpink and richly fragrant.

'Alfred de Dalmas', equally well known as 'Mousseline', is one of the Moss roses that repeat blossoming during the growing season. Buds are covered in greenish brown mossing and open to pale pink, midsize, sweetly scented blossoms.

'Salet' is another faithfully reblooming Moss rose. Although its bush is so lanky that it demands support and despite the fact that mossing is only light, the clear soft pink blossoms are irresistibly scented.

If flower size is important to you (the bigger the better), take a look at 'Gloire des Mousseux', which produces the largest blossoms of all Moss roses. The clear pink

'salet'

blooms are crammed with quartered petals that reflex as they age, but they never lose their perfume.

If bush size appeals to you, consider 'William Lobb', a Moss rose so vigorous that support is required for bushes in the ground after only two years. The blossoms are worth any such trouble—robustly fragrant and colored from purple to gray, with a lighter color on each petal's reverse.

If clear coloring appeals to you, by all means take a gander at 'Henri Martin', whose blossoms are as pure a crimson as any rose of any age. Mossing is sparse and fragrance is slight, but the hips that form in fall are a great plus.

Gardeners who appreciate darkly colored blooms should check out 'Nuits de Young', whose buds are so purple that they look black. As flowers mature, petals unfurl to reveal a boss of golden yellow stamens.

Landscapers are fond of 'Marechal Davoust', which produces shapely shrubs that gracefully arch their rosebuds covered in greenish brown moss. Blossoms range in color from purple to mauve, but all are strongly fragrant and contain green button-eyed centers.

Diminutive Moss roses exist, too, such as 'Little Gem'. Its fragrant crimson blossoms are formed like pompons and occur over an extended period of bloom. All parts of the plant (even the stems) are heavily mossed.

'henri martin'

3

REBLOOMING ROSES

As mentioned in the chapter on Species roses, those from Oriental Asia were famed for their enviable ability to repeat blossoming during summer. Hybridizers couldn't wait to get their hands on varieties of R. chinensis, *the China rose. Then, late in the 18th century, word reached Europe that there were four descendants of* R. chinensis *whose pollen was so potent that they had been nicknamed "stud roses."*

Rosedom would have been hard put to find a greater benefactress to the genus than Empress Josephine Bonaparte, who was passionate about roses and wanted to help in the creation of new rose varieties. Her determination was so intense that she exercised her influence to get these supposed stud roses out of China even while the Napoleonic Wars were waging.

Alas, Josephine and her would-be rose breeders were disappointed with early efforts at hybridizing. Even when the Chinese studs were crossed with the finest European varieties available, nothing spectacular occurred. Not only were blooms disappointing, plants stubbornly flowered only once each year.

Finally, rose breeders struck paydirt when they decided to cross the lackluster offspring with the original Chinese varieties. By the time sufficient pollen

'nuits de young'

had been crossed and recrossed, the four stud roses had sired five new families of roses: Chinas, Portlands, Bourbons, Hybrid Perpetuals, and Teas.

china roses

China roses are distinguished by airy growth habits and sparse foliage. Compared with their ancestors, blooms are meager, too. Whereas the blooms of antique roses are intricately (often precisely) formed, those of China roses are relatively shapeless. Despite such seeming disappointments, however, Chinas possess undeniable naive charm, and the fact that they rebloom all summer long is a huge plus.

Landscapers are fond of China roses and use them often precisely because of their faults. Since growth is diaphanous and foliage thin, many varieties blend well into mixed borders, filling in gaps but never dominating the landscape.

'Parsons' Pink China', far better known as 'Old Blush', is not only the most famous of the original four stud roses, it's also the prettiest and the one most comfortably at home in most gardens. Vigorous plants freely produce informal clusters of dainty pink blossoms that intensify in color as they age. Fragrance is notable, too, and often likened to that of sweet peas because of a hint of vanilla in an otherwise sophisticated rosy bouquet.

Some years after it first grew as a conventional shrub, 'Old Blush' spontaneously developed a mutation that preferred to climb rather than hover at ground

'old bush'

level. Many rosarians, myself included, consider the climbing sport to be superior to the conventional plant.

Also famous among the China roses is 'Gloire Des Rosomanes', ubiquitously known as 'Ragged Robin', not so much for the plant itself but rather because it was once the most popular understock (the rose variety onto which other rose hybrids are grafted) in commerce. Early in the 20th century, 'Ragged Robin' proved to have such a rugged root structure that the variety lost all value for its flowers—a pity, since its semidouble blossoms are a cheerful shade of crimson. Today other rose varieties have emerged as favorites for rootstock and 'Ragged Robin' has been returned to the landscape.

My personal favorite China rose is 'Mutabilis', sometimes called the butter-fly rose because, when in full bloom, plants appear to be landing pads for masses of dainty butterflies. Flowers undergo a dramatic change in coloring as they mature. Buds that are shades of honey-copper develop into pink blossoms that eventually turn crimson. When plants are in full bloom, all colors are apparent at once.

An oddity among China roses is 'Viridiflora', better known as the green rose. Insanely popular among flower arrangers, 'Viridiflora' doesn't actually "bloom"; it masses green sepals so abundantly that they give the effect of blossoms. Personally, I wouldn't consider growing 'Viridiflora', but then I'm not an arranger.

I will always grow 'Gold of Ophir', however, and not just because it was the favorite rose of my late friend M.F.K. Fisher, who said its blooming bounty looked

'mutabilis'

"like a moon on fire." Sentiment aside, 'Gold of Ophir' is not merely a thoroughly satisfactory climbing rose, it also tolerates as much shade as any rose I know.

Gardeners in search of plants that hover close to the ground have several China roses from which to choose. The two most popular are 'Cramoisi Superieur', which gathers its nonfading, clear red flowers in clusters, and 'Fabvier', which rarely grows taller than 2 feet but seldom stops blossoming bright red flowers streaked with white.

portland roses

At the dawn of the 19th century, the Duchess of Portland imported a rose from Italy that was reputed to bloom throughout the summer. *R. paestana*, also known as 'Scarlet Four Seasons' Rose', so thrilled the duchess that she sent plants to Andre Dupont, head gardener at Malmaison, home to Empress Josephine's massive collection of roses.

Josephine and her prestigious staff were so impressed with their gift that they renamed the rose 'Duchess of Portland', and hybridizers were soon to have their way with its pollen, producing scads of hybrids in the process. Only a few remain in commerce today.

The blooms of Portland roses resemble their Damask ancestors more than anything else, except that their stems are notably shorter. As if to compensate for their short stems, the shrubs are vigorous, upright (usually to between 3 and 4 feet), and compact. Foliage is plentiful and particularly dense just under each blossom—what Britain's esteemed rosarian Graham Stuart Thomas eloquently labels a "shoulder of leaves."

'gold of ophir'

Not from sentiment alone, 'Portland Rose', the original variety named for the Duchess of Portland, remains in commerce. Although plants rarely grow taller than 3 feet, they flower with masses of blossoms whose cerise red petals surround a healthy clump of prominent bright yellow stamens. Fragrance is virtually indistinguishable from that of several members of the Damask family of roses.

'Comte de Chambord' is surely the most popular Portland rose, and for sound reasons; not simply because shrubs grow vigorously to 4 feet with almost as much girth, but also since blossoms are thoroughly winning—fully double, deep pink fading to lilac, and sumptuously perfumed. Characteristic of the family, foliage grows smack up to the blossoms, lending them elegant architectural support.

Although shorter and not as floriferous as 'Comte de Chambord', 'Jacques Cartier' is considered by many rose enthusiasts to be the finest member of the Portland family of roses. I believe that honor is due solely to the perfection of its blossoms— clear pink, heavily petaled, lovingly shaped, and deeply fragrant.

'Blanc de Vibert' is the Portland of choice for gardeners fond of white roses. Not only do blossoms occur over a long season, they're also winningly cupped, heavily petaled, and redolent of perfume usually reserved for Damask roses.

'Rose du Roi' may not be particularly robust (it's sometimes downright straggly), but it blooms freely and repeats well. Best of all are the richly scented blossoms themselves—fully double, but loosely formed of red petals mottled purple.

'duchess of portland'

Nearing the middle of the 19th century, Mother Nature played a wondrous trick on residents of the Ile de Bourbon who liked to surround their dwellings with mixed hedges of *R. chinensis* and *R. damascena*. With assistance only from bees and other pollinators of nature, a variety emerged that had the best qualities of both of its parents.

Hips that formed from the discovery were sent to the head gardener of King Louis-Philippe, who raised a seedling he named 'Rosier de l'Ile de Bourbon'. Realizing its potential, hybridizers crossed the "new" rose with popular varieties of the time, and the Bourbon family of roses was born.

What a find! Even today, horticulturists worldwide agree that the Bourbons were the true forerunners of roses that unite the best of two rose worlds—the old and the new. Like heirloom roses, Bourbons are wondrously colored and packed with fragrant petals; like modern roses, Bourbons blossom from early summer through fall.

The majority of Bourbon hybrids form large shrubs that appreciate support for their weighty canes, making them ideal candidates for short climbers and fence huggers. Bourbons are also the first family of roses for whom precise parentage was listed (prior to Bourbons, it seemingly never occurred to rose breeders that careful recordings of pollination crossings might someday prove useful).

'Madame Isaac Pereire' is perhaps the most famous Bourbon rose because of her outrageous perfume. Many fragrance aficionados claim that this is the most

'madame isaac pereire'

fragrant rose in the world, but that's a close call. Apart from an unarguable scent, 'Madame Isaac Pereire' has some additional fine qualities going for it, not the least of which are the unusually large and dramatically colored blooms. The huge blossoms are hot pink shaded magenta and undergo dramatic alterations in form as they mature. Buds are cupped at first; then as the petals begin to unfurl, they reflex to form quartered blossoms that reach 6-inch spans. Just before a button-eyed center is revealed, the petals fade at their edges, making the blooms two-tone hot pink.

Grown as a conventional shrub, plants may reach 7 feet. Cultivated as a climber, which she prefers, the Madame may well cover 18 feet. Either way, plants are well clothed in thick, deep green foliage. Flowering is more or less constant over summer. The first bloom is outrageous, followed by a smattering of blossoms throughout summer and a good repeat in fall.

A few years after it was introduced, 'Madame Isaac Pereire' produced a sport, 'Madame Ernest Calvat', that is similar to its parent in every way except bloom color, which in this case is light to medium pink. Fragrance may not be quite as heady, but it's still plenty strong.

Other Bourbon roses produced sports, too, some outclassing their natural parent. 'Madame Pierre Oger', for instance, produces some of the most refined blossoms of all Bourbons—chalice-shaped, pinky beige flowers that resemble translucent water lilies. Alas, like its mother 'La Reine Victoria', 'Madame Pierre Oger' has a marked affinity for blackspot.

'madame ernest calvat'

Similarly, 'Bourbon Queen', a sturdy plant bearing nicely scented, rose-pink blossoms with crinkled petals, produced a sport named 'Prince Charles', the most darkly colored member of the entire family. Blooms start out purple and then fade to rich lilac, the petals heavily veined crimson.

'Souvenir de la Malmaison', named to honor the chateau where Josephine held court, is available both as a bush and as a climber, the latter being the better form. Conventional shrubs have a sprawling growth habit and rarely grow taller than 3 feet. The climbing version, however, is vigorous and strong enough to support the large, delicate, blush-pink blossoms that carry a classic Tea rose scent.

'Coupe d'Hebe' is another family member that grows better as a climber than as a conventional shrub. Owing to their natural upright growth habit, if left unstaked, shrubs become awkward. Given support, plants are comfortable producing fragrant, pale to rich pink, globular flowers. Foliage is a lighter shade of green than that of most Bourbon roses and is also susceptible to mildew.

'Boule de Neige' is the Bourbon of choice for gardeners fond of creamy white. When flowers first appear, one might worry that the wrong variety has been planted, because they're nowhere near white. Outside petals are flushed with pink and crimson, but as they mature, blossoms formed in clusters turn white. Perfume is rich all the while.

Striped roses are popular no matter what their age, and no family (except perhaps the Gallicas) has a finer striped variety than the Bourbon rose 'Honorine de

'la reine victoria'

Brabant'. Large blossoms are basically baby pink but are lovingly streaked with soft shades of light purple, lilac, and mauve. Foliage is plentiful and stems are relatively thornless.

Although the stripes of 'Variegata di Bologna' are far less subtle than those of 'Honorine de Brabant', they're appealingly dramatic and blooms are magnificently scented. Base color is creamy white, but blossoms are stunningly striped with blotches of crimson and purple, no two alike. Shrubs grow to 5 to 6 feet, but climbers scramble to 10 feet.

hybrid perpetual roses

When gardening became fashionable in the mid-19th century, Hybrid Perpetual roses were bred on demand. Determined to outdo Mrs. Whozis at the next garden show, Mrs. Whatzis told rose hybridizers exactly what she wanted—prizewinning blossoms developing from picture-perfect buds. Never mind what the plants looked like, the flowers were the ticket.

After acknowledging that rose hybridizing is something of a crapshoot anyway, breeders adopted a what-the-heck attitude and crossed pollen from every established variety they could grab.

New varieties were born, all right—more than 3,000 of them, several of which produced buds and blooms that were precisely what exhibitors had in mind. The plants on which they were borne, however, were another matter. In fact, because of their tall, clumsy growth habits, these skyscrapers could no longer be called shrubs.

'boule de neige'

Worse yet, several were also sickly and prone to common rose ailments such as powdery mildew, and they grew far too tall for most gardens. Consequently, today few rose suppliers carry more than a handful of Hybrid Perpetuals, some varieties strictly out of sentiment.

The most notorious of all Hybrid Perpetual roses got off to a shaky start toward fame. 'Mme Ferdinand Jamin', hybridized in France in 1875, enjoyed moderate success in Europe. When it was sent to the United States in 1882, it was a flop; not because of the variety itself, growers thought, but rather because of its name. Once the name was changed to 'American Beauty', the variety raged toward success. It even became the official floral symbol for Washington, D.C.

The reason 'American Beauty' remains popular is due entirely to its blossoms, which are cupped and bright carmine and occur on particularly long cutting stems. Its bush, however, exhibits a persistent affinity for powdery mildew.

My pet among Hybrid Perpetuals is 'Paul Neyron'. He outclasses 'American Beauty' easily by a mile. First, unlike its ailing sibling, 'Paul Neyron' is quite resistant to disease and the blooms have to be seen to be believed—fragrant blossoms that reach dinner-plate proportions, with pink and lilac petals swirling out of control.

Another Hybrid Perpetual with no time for disease is 'Baronne Prevost', who also produces comely blossoms that appear to be of an older era than they actually are (it was introduced in 1842). Shrubs grow to 4 feet all around and the tough foliage is an appealing shade of midgreen.

'american beauty'

'Frau Karl Druschki', introduced in 1901, was the world's favorite white rose for years despite the fact that it hasn't a whiff of scent and its blossoms pout when the weather is damp. When the weather is warm, however, blossoms are fabulous—large, globular, and pure white except for a kiss of lemon at the base of each petal. Foliage is light green and appears tough even though it actually isn't.

'Ferdinand Pichard' is the striped member of the Hybrid Perpetual family. Petals have a pink base color but are madly striped crimson and white. Blossoms are only medium-size, but they're fragrant and prolific. Foliage is abundant and a rich shade of green.

Henry Bennett, the trendsetter for roses in Victorian and Edwardian land-scapes, considered 'Mrs. John Laing' his hybridizing triumph, and it's easy to see (and smell) why. Blossoms are silvery pink and deeply fragrant and appear regularly throughout summer. The plant is notable, too, growing to about 4 feet but not as wide, making it an easily manageable shrub.

If sheer beauty of flower appeals strongly to you and fragrance doesn't make much difference, by all means consider 'Baroness Rothschild', whose blossoms are perfectly formed of soft pink petals with a silky texture. Although the gray-green foliage is abundant and grows smack-dab up to the blossoms, it is no stranger to common rose infestations.

Gardeners fond of 'Reine des Violettes' can't seem to get enough of it, and I'm certain it's due to color—blossoms begin life velvety purple and later fade to soft

baronne prevost

violet. Fragrance could also be a factor, since 'Reine des Violettes' is richly perfumed. Be forewarned, however, that blossoms shatter and drop their petals almost immediately after reaching full maturity.

tea roses

From crosses made between Bourbon and Noisette roses and a couple of the original stud roses from China, the Tea rose was born. Like man, the first one was named 'Adam'.

From 'Adam' onward, it was easy to see that a whole new world of roses was about to reveal itself. These Tea roses weren't the ticket to rose utopia, however; although the blooms were beautiful and lovingly formed, their bushes were weak and many varieties had deadly reaction to cold. But they were deliciously fragrant, redolent of a scent also dubbed Tea. For the many people who complain that Tea roses don't smell like tea at all, it should be noted that that wasn't how the name was born. The "tea" derives from the fact that the scent of these roses was similar to that of the wood used to make the crates that once held tea leaves during shipment from the Far East.

Unlike their modern offspring, Tea roses don't take well to severe winter pruning; only dead and spindly wood should be taken from bushes. Despite their relatively delicate nature, certain Tea roses have stood the test of time.

For three reasons, my favorite is 'Catherine Mermet'. First, color. Immature petals are blush pink with lilac edges. As they mature, petals turn an almost uniform soft shade of beige. Second, fragrance—classic Tea rose scent. Third, and plenty

'reine des violettes'

important, vase life. Properly conditioned after harvesting (stems recut under water, then placed in hot water to which bleach and preservatives have been added), blossoms of 'Catherine Mermet' last a seeming eternity in a vase. In recognition of such lasting power, 'Catherine Mermet' is sometimes cultivated as a greenhouse variety for the cut-flower trade.

'Bridesmaid', a sport of 'Catherine Mermet', is similar to her mother in all regards except bloom color. Here, blossoms are decidedly pink, not pinky-beige.

'Lady Hillingdon', hybridized in 1910, is almost as popular as when it was introduced, in part because seven years after it grew only as a bush, it produced a climbing sport that has outsold its parent. Grown either way, it bears blooms that are knockouts—apricot-yellow and fragrant as all get-out. Other parts of the plant are well-colored, too. Foliage is glossy and handsomely shaded purplish-green, and new wood is plum-colored. Somewhat sensitive to cold, 'Lady Hillingdon' is labeled "moderately hardy."

Another Tea rose that grows either as a shrub or as a climber, but is thoroughly resistant to winter, is 'Archiduc Joseph'. Blossoms that flatten as they mature are composed of purple and pink petals surrounding centers of pale yellow stamens. Foliage is ample, but thorns are few.

'Duchesse de Brabant', introduced in 1857, is among the most fragrant of all Tea roses. Blooms are large, cupped, clear to rose-pink, and sumptuously perfumed. Blossoming is more or less continuous from early summer through fall.

'archiduc joseph'

'Maman Cochet' was once a firebreather at the exhibition table. Globular buds that start out with little promise mature into buxom blossoms of multishaded pink petals with distinct lemon-yellow markings. Bushes sport leathery green foliage and few thorns. As was common for heirloom roses, 'Maman Cochet' developed a sport, in this case a white one. 'White Maman Cochet' is like its parent in every way except color; this time creamy white, flushed pink.

'Safrano' is such a treasured Tea rose that gardeners put up with it being tender to cold (in support of the variety, I must point out that it makes a fine container plant, easily afforded winter protection). Surely the most endearing charm of 'Safrano' is the color of its blossoms—saffron yellow, tinged apricot. The heady fragrance doesn't hurt one bit.

The world of heirloom roses was brought to an abrupt halt in 1867, when Guillot of France hybridized 'La France', generally considered to be the first Hybrid Tea rose. Then the rose world was off and running, and thousands of hybrids were soon to emerge. They'd never have done so, however, without the genes of their sturdy ancestors.

'maman cochet' in bucket

4

P L A N T I N G

Although many heirloom roses demand considerably less care than do modern hybrids, an equal number are just as fussy over where and in what they grow. The general rule of thumb is that the older the rose variety, the less care it will probably need, including where and how it's planted.

Many Species roses, for instance, may well not know how to respond if afforded the luxurious planting techniques necessary for modern roses. Although I've never proved so myself, I doubt that *R. palustris*, the swamp rose, would know how to behave if drainage were made perfect. Similarly, I doubt that *R. setigera*, the prairie rose, could fathom how to handle ample summer waterings.

Species roses came to be in the first place because they grew quite happily without anybody fussing over them. They still will; don't coddle them.

As breeders created new roses on their way to hybridizing Hybrid Teas, however, cross-pollinators unwittingly introduced varieties that demanded considerably more care than did their Species grandparents. The reblooming Hybrid Perpetual family, for instance, is chock-full of members that are every bit as demanding as the prissiest of modern Hybrid Teas.

'safrano'

In between these two extremes are countless varieties of roses that may not actually require coddling. Nevertheless, because they so obviously appreciate it, as proved by exemplary growth and bountiful bloom, I give them some, especially when I plant them.

I believe that if you have any intention of keeping a rose, you must give it a good home, preferably when its bushes are bareroot. Considering how inexpensive rosebushes are, providing them with comfortable surroundings seems like a mere token repayment for the rewards you're destined to reap.

First, give rosebushes as sunny a location as possible, at least five hours of full sun each day. While it's true that certain heirloom roses will tolerate considerable shade, roses are basically sun-lovers. Second, try to plant in areas sheltered from wind and in close proximity to ample sources of water. Finally, afford rosebushes the best drainage you can.

Begin by digging a hole 2 feet wide and 18 inches deep. If you have any doubt that the soil you remove is anything less than good garden soil (preferably loam), get rid of it and plan to refill the hole with a commercially available all-purpose soil to which organic nutrients (peat moss, aged manure, or compost) can be added. Next, fill the hole with water and see if it takes longer than an hour to drain. If it does, dig 6 to 8 inches deeper and fill the new depth with gravel.

'rose du roi'

Once you're satisfied that the hole will continue to drain quickly and thoroughly, make a mound of soil (either that which you removed or what you purchased) at the bottom of the hole and pack the soil to form a tepee. Nestle the roots of your bareroot rosebush over the tepee and then, bit by bit, refill the rest of the hole with soil and pat the soil into place. Water to soak.

Finally, to prevent winds from parching new canes, mound your newly planted bareroot bush with materials you intend to employ later as mulch—compost, wood (preferably fir) shavings, thoroughly aged manure (fowl is best, chicken or turkey), or, even better, a combination of all three.

Bushes purchased in containers from reputable nurseries come with soil in which roses like to grow. Depending on how long the plant has been in the container, the soil around it will be more or less loose (the longer it's in the container, the firmer the soil).

Whether in the ground or in a pot, newly planted bareroot roses quickly develop massive hairlike root systems. If these webs are sufficiently formed to hold the soil intact after a pot-grown plant is tapped out of its container, plant the bush as is, keeping as much of the container soil as possible. If the roots haven't yet developed sufficiently to keep the soil in place, treat the bush as you would if it were bareroot, tepee and all.

'baroness rothschild'

Because so many heirloom roses grow well on their own roots, you'll sometimes be offered them that way; alternatively, they may have been budded onto rootstock. There are advantages to both ways of growing rosebushes, but experience is proving more conclusively that own-root roses are the way to grow.

First, roses growing on their own roots never develop suckers (undesirable growth from the rootstock onto which hybrids are budded). Second, own-root roses are more winter-hardy. Finally, roses growing on their own roots don't develop viruses, the way budded roses often do.

In fact, the only drawback I know to own-root roses is that some varieties grow out of bounds. I've seen so for myself, with a bed of 'Complicata' rosebushes, half budded and half growing on their own roots. In three years, the own-root plants were fountainous and could no longer be constrained in the spaces I had afforded them. The budded siblings, however, remained controllably compact. If gargantuan growth is no threat to your garden, when offered the choice, buy plants growing on their own roots.

'ferdinand pichard'

5

M A I N T A I N I N G

How much care an heirloom rose requires follows the same general rule as that for planting—the older the variety, the less fuss necessary. Once hybridizers learned how to make roses rebloom, however, they simultaneously created nourishment needs (the more a rose variety flowers, the more food it requires between crops).

I don't fertilize Species roses at all. The nutrients leached yearly from a comfy blanket of well-aged manure provide all the nourishment they seem to need.

Similarly, I don't pamper antique roses (the five distinct families developed just prior to roses that rebloomed), although I go a step further than merely supplying mulch. Once winter is officially over and plants have begun to develop foliage, I also feed each mature bush with a fertilizer concentrated in nitrogen, such as ammonium sulfate or calcium nitrate. One month later, I give each bush 3/4 cup of Epsom salts. Watering, which should take place immediately after each feeding, should be deep and thorough.

Otherwise, for the bulk of the season, I just make certain that plants are never stressed from thirst and that the blankets of mulch haven't entirely decomposed (if they have, I add additional mulch, but nothing more).

'madame pierre oger'

There are exceptions to these seemingly meager tokens of care. If a variety seems less robust than it should, in midsummer I feed it either with doses of fish emulsion at the rate of 1 tablespoon per gallon of water or with a granular, water-soluble, balanced fertilizer such as 10-10-10, 15-15-15, or 20-20-20, always at the manufacturer's suggested application rate.

If I gardened where winters weren't sufficiently severe to ensure dormancy, toward the end of the growing season I might feed each bush a meal of 0-10-10 to make certain that wood hardens off before pruning time.

The care I offer rosebushes accelerates markedly for roses that rebloom, and it's only good common sense to give it. When you consider how much effort it takes for bushes to produce a crop of blossoms, it seems obvious that they'd appreciate nutrients just after they breathe a sigh of relief.

In addition to the care I just described for antique roses, I give reblooming roses extra food during the growing season. Once a month during summer, I feed each mature bush with a well-balanced fertilizer. When that seems insufficient (relative to the plant's showy output), I supplement the diet with feedings of fish emulsion and also with an extra dose of Epsom salts.

Like many rosarians fond of Heirloom roses, I'm not fond of spraying. So I don't. My heirloom roses are planted in the landscape, often near vegetables and herbs

'comte de chambord'

that I wouldn't dream of subjecting to chemicals because I intend to eat them at some point. Since I refuse to spray, however, I can't grow all the varieties mentioned in this book. As hybridizers got closer to breeding Hybrid Tea roses (which frequently require painstaking care, including regular spraying), in order to create perfection in bloom, they sacrificed overall plant health. Many members of the Hybrid Perpetual family and the clan of Tea roses, for instance, are every bit as susceptible to common rose ailments as are their modern offspring. I avoid them.

My feeding program for heirloom roses may seem stingy, but my watering program won't, although that's largely because where I grow roses, there is virtually no rainfall during summer months. I flood rose beds at least once a week during summer, more often when heat turns intense.

It's more important to water deeply than to water often. Surface watering may increase feeder roots (which develop no matter how you water), but only deep soakings encourage strong root development. Also, try to irrigate roses without watering them from overhead. Wet foliage invites disease.

'petite de hollande'

6

H A R V E S T I N G

Although heirloom roses aren't generally considered ideal cut flowers, the way modern hybrids are, many varieties produce superb blossoms for enjoying indoors. The trick is to harvest the blooms at the right time and to condition them for maximum vase life.

Because of their high petal count, heirloom roses often produce blossoms that have an extended life, one far beyond that of their modern offspring. That entire life cannot always be enjoyed in a vase, however. Cut too soon, blossoms will refuse to develop further, thereby calling a halt to potential showiness.

The heavier the petalage of the rose, the longer it must mature on its bush before being cut. The heavily petaled Centifolia rose 'Fantin-Latour', for example, can't be harvested before it has reached its half-open stage or it won't mature further. Similarly, if expected to fully unfurl their many petals, few Bourbon roses can be cut in bud.

Conversely, roses light on petals (especially single-petaled varieties) can be cut near the bud stage. Even certain Species roses make good cut flowers, although none I've grown have particularly extended vase life. Varieties with 20 or fewer petals can be cut while fairly tight in bud with realistic expectations of full maturity.

If you grow roses specifically because you want to enjoy their blossoms as cut

'fantin-latour'

flowers, be forewarned that the majority of heirloom roses have short stems. Members of the Portland family, for instance, are known for producing magnificent blooms on comparatively puny stems. This does not spell doom for such roses as cut flowers; it merely limits the height for arranging them (sometimes an advantage, as with dining table centerpieces).

I recommend that you cut rose blossoms in either early morning or late afternoon, when plants retain maximum moisture, and that you not take a bucket of water along on your way to harvest. Besides running the risk of sloshing the entire bucket on your feet, you don't really do rose blossoms a favor by plunking them into water as soon as they're cut; it's the care you give them later that matters.

Instead of a bucket, use a garden wicker basket or trug and gently layer cut rose blossoms in it, being careful not to compress petals by laying blooms on top of each other. Then, indoors, using the same shears you used to cut the blossoms from their bushes, recut the stems under water.

Rather than making cuts under running water from the kitchen sink (which will work, but is messy), plunge the stems into a small bowl of water and recut 1/4 inch off their stems. Then put the harvested blossoms into a container of hot water (that from the kitchen tap will do) to which, per quart, two or three drops of bleach and 3/4 teaspoon of floral preservatives (if you have none on hand, use sugar) have been added.

If you've never recut stems under water, try it; you'll be amazed at how long you can extend the vase life of garden roses.

'jacques cartier'

7

P R U N I N G

There are two distinct schools of thought on when it's best to prune roses that bloom only once each year. Some believe that pruning should take place immediately after plants flower; others maintain that shrubs should be pruned only when dormant. At the risk of seeming like I'm copping out on the debate, I do both, but my approach to pruning heirloom roses is even more unconventional.

I don't prune Species or antique roses at all for the first three years they're in the ground (some not until after their fifth year). Once plants have reached the approximate size I'm looking for, then I begin to prune them into the precise shape I'm after. Remember that many of these roses mature into gargantuan plants that don't respond to conventional pruning rules no matter what your general approach.

The reason I don't make all pruning cuts immediately after flowering is that foliage is so abundant that it camouflages the places where precise pruning cuts should be made. Consequently, after flowering, I remove only wood that has proved to be unproductive or that looks like it's on the brink of becoming so (dead and twiggy growth should be removed anytime it's spotted, regardless of the season). Then, when plants are dormant, I consider additional pruning.

'rosa multiflora carnea'

I prune reblooming roses in winter, the same time I prune my modern roses. Although I don't prune them as hard as I do their modern offspring, I follow the same general guidelines and cut back canes to two-thirds (occasionally one-half) of their pre-pruned height.

Mother Nature is willing to give you a hand at making pruning easier when plants are dormant. Two weeks before you intend to prune them, remove all foliage from the bushes. In another two weeks, dormant eyes will swell and turn red, pinpointing the exact spots where judicious pruning cuts should be made. Look for dormant eyes facing outward from the center of the bush and make pruning cuts $1/4$ inch above them.

When whole canes should be removed from plants, cut them off at their bases (just above the bud union for varieties that are budded onto rootstock; at ground level for varieties growing on their own roots).

Climbing and Rambling roses should be left unpruned for their first couple of years in the ground. The goal is to coax plants upward to what they're intended to scramble over. For the first few years, remove only dead or spindly wood. Then keep an eye on retaining the canes you need to shape the plant. Remember also that, eventually, you want the tips of Climbing and Rambling roses to point downward, encouraging sap to flow along the entire length of the canes, resulting in floriferous bloom.

The very thought of pruning some rampant heirloom roses is enough to induce a splitting headache (so is the possibility of merely defoliating them). I've planted some Species roses and heirloom Ramblers, for instance, because they tend to gobble up whatever fence, stump, even shed, I've planted them next to. For as long as I can resist, I don't prune them at all, at most cutting off the tips of their growth while the plants are dormant. Eventually, however, you have no choice but to remove whole canes because new basal growth will be choked out unless old wood is first removed. Steel yourself, and get rid of it.

Although I've confessed to not spraying my heirloom roses with chemicals during their growing season because I grow them in close proximity to edible plants, I make an exception in winter and strongly urge you to do the same, by employing dormant-spray materials.

Dormant sprays are specially formulated to clean up any diseases a bush may be harboring. Most spray concentrates have a base of sulfur or copper, both known to effectively eradicate common rose diseases, and all are safe and easy to use. Since dormant sprays burn foliage, they are meant to be applied only when bushes are dormant and leafless.

Bushes stripped of foliage in anticipation of pruning are ideal candidates for dormant sprays. While you're at it, spray the soil around the plants as well. Disease spores are often harbored in fallen leaves, cuttings, and mulch. Dormant sprays knock them flat. Your roses will bless you for the effort.

I N D E X